The Great Ground Plan -

A Study of the True Pyramids of Egypt

Jani Laasonen

THE GREAT GROUND PLAN -
A STUDY OF THE TRUE PYRAMIDS OF EGYPT

Previously Published (in Finnish)

<u>Kaaos ja Kosmos -kirjasarja:</u>

Osa 1: Kaaos ja Ajan Henki (also known as: Zeitgeist – Ajan henki)

Osa 2: Kosmos ja Totuuden Tie

<u>Egyptin todelliset pyramidit -kirjasarja:</u>

Osa 1: Egyptin Suuren pyramidin tutkimuksen historia

Osa 2: Egyptin todellisten pyramidien geometria

Osa 3: Rajapatsas

Blogs

https://thegreatgroundplan.blogspot.com/   (in English)
http://resurssipohjainentalous.blogspot.com/   (in Finnish)
https://rajapatsas.blogspot.com/   (in Finnish)

e-mail: greatgroundplan@gmail.com

Kustantaja: BoD – Books on Demand, Helsinki, Suomi

Valmistaja: BoD – Books on Demand, Norderstedt, Saksa

ISBN: 978-952-802-267-1

Content

Introduction

My research on the pyramids started few years ago, as I got interested in the fascinating geometry of the Great Pyramid of Giza. I was lured in by the proportions of the Great Pyramid, which are quite unique, for its shape represents very accurately two timeless mathematical constants: pi ($\pi \approx 3.142$) and phi ($\phi \approx 0.618$ or $\varphi \approx 1.618$). Their occurrence together in such a significant construction in such a sophisticated way seemed to be more than just a coincidence, so I decided to investigate the subject a little more. Quite soon I started making mathematical discoveries that baffled me and captivated my attention for years to come. Eventually my main focus concentrated primarily on these three aspects:

1. The unit of measure upon which the true pyramids were built called "The royal cubit" and its connection to modern meter through the geometry of a circle divided by twelve.
2. The ground plans of true pyramids of Egypt and the clear mathematical plan they represent.
3. Pyramid architecture that follows this same mathematical plan.

But before we go any further, we need to define what is a true pyramid. A true pyramid is a pyramid, that follows these five characteristics:

- It is regarded by modern Egyptologists as 4th dynasty pyramid.
- It has a square base that is aligned very precisely with the four cardinal points of compass.
- It was built to last: Despite being built nearly 5,000 years ago it still represents almost flawless geometry.
- No mummies, funerary scriptures, funerary art or any grave goods have ever been found inside of it.
- It was designed and built in royal cubits (1 royal cubit = 0.5236 meters).

There are only five pyramids in Egypt that meet all these five requirements. Three of them are in Giza and two of them in Dahshur. In this study, I name these five true pyramids from north to south with numbers from one to five (1-5) so that the northernmost pyramid (The Great Pyramid of Giza) is the 1st true pyramid and the southernmost pyramid (The Bent Pyramid of Dahshur) is the 5th true pyramid.

In this book will be shown how true pyramids form three different ground plans on map: one to Giza, one to Dahshur, and finally the Great Ground Plan comprising all five true pyramids of Egypt. The side lengths and the diagonals of these ground plans follow clear mathematical pattern, which can no longer be mere accident, but a sign of systematic planning.

As this research seeks to follow the procedure of a scientific survey, the aim is to present the results in the most straightforward and unambiguous way possible, so that they are easy to peer review and replicate. The study involves measuring long distances, for which purpose is used a tool called Google Earth. No other tools are needed.

This book is based on previous research written in Finnish. If the content seems interesting, one might also get acquainted with the original study at: https://rajapatsas.blogspot.com/. With the help of free translation tools, one can get quite good idea of the content, even if Finnish is not one's mother tongue.

Geometrical Connection Between Modern Meter and Ancient Cubit

The Great Pyramid – like all the other true pyramids - was built by using a standard of measure called royal cubit. Signs of its use can be found throughout the structures of all true pyramids. Sir Flinders Petrie made the first scientifically valid estimate of cubit's exact length in the 1880s while doing a triangulation survey of the whole Giza pyramid area. According to his research he estimated cubit's length to be some 20.63 inches (0.524 meters) long.

Over hundred years later, in 1992-1993, a German engineer Rudolf Gantenbrink explored the narrow "air shafts" of the Great Pyramid with the help of crawler robots. During this process, he made the first accurate 3D modeling of the whole Great Pyramid. Based on his measurements, he determined the exact length of the cubit to be: 0.5236 meters, which means 52 centimeters and 3.6 millimeters. This is extremely accurate measurement for a unit of measure that existed some 5,000 years ago. It tells something about the passion and dedication that scientists around the world have always felt for the true pyramids and the mystery of their construction.

The thing that caught my eye with the ancient cubit was the fact that its exact length could be derived directly from the modern meter by drawing a circle with a radius of exactly one meter and then dividing the circumference by twelve. The length of one royal cubit is $1/12^{th}$ of the length of the circumference of a circle with a radius of one meter.

Circle divided by twelve is very old symbol of divine perfection. We all know this division, because it bears a very special meaning in our culture. For example: zodiac and 12 constellations, clock face and 12 hours, musical scale and 12 notes, year and 12 months, flag and 12 stars, atom and 12 elementary particles, teacher and 12 students, people and 12 tribes, hero and 12 feats, and so on. All of these symbols follow the same pattern: there is one whole, that is divided by twelve. Now we can add one more thing to the list: unit circle with a radius of one meter divided by 12 cubits.

Radius of the circle = 1 meter
Circumference of the circle = τ = 2π = 6,283... meters = 12 cubits
1/12 of the circumference of the circle: τ/12 = 0,5236 meters = 1 cubit

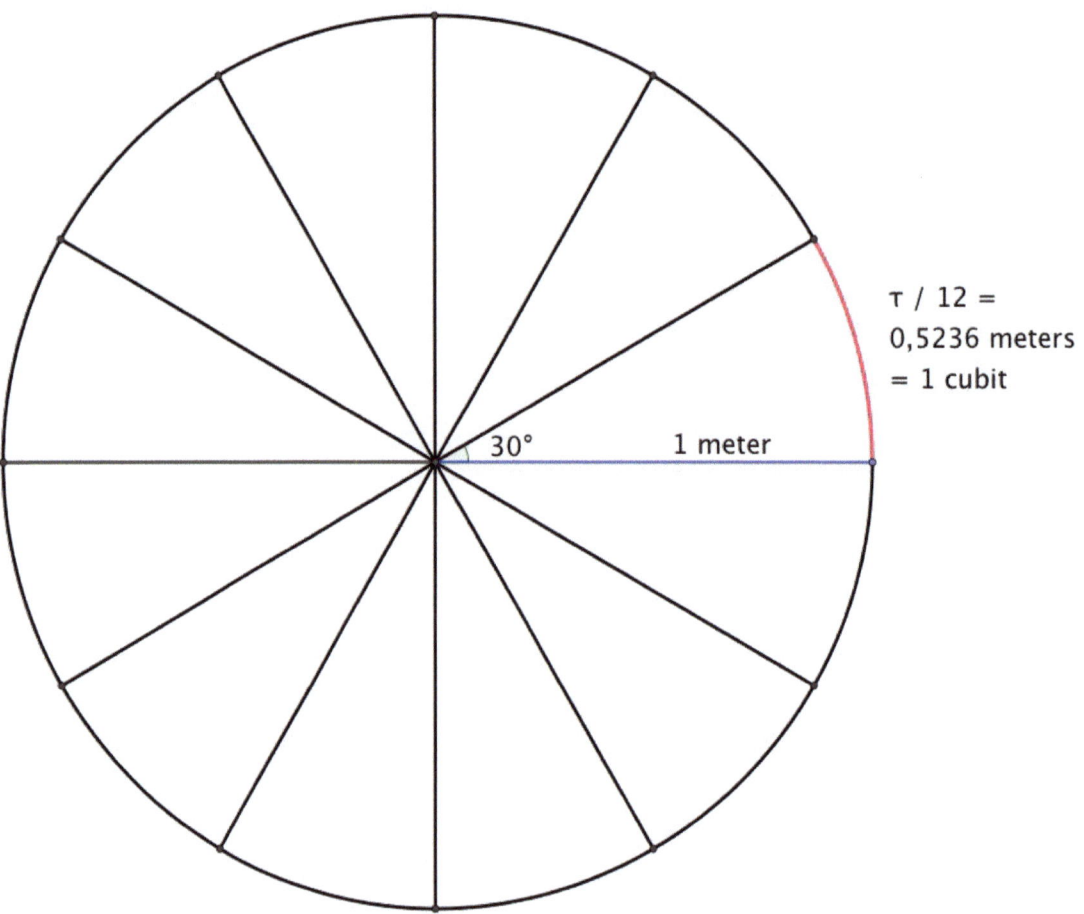

τ / 12 =
0,5236 meters
= 1 cubit

30°   1 meter

When drawing a circle with a radius of exactly one meter, the result is a perimeter of
2π or tau (τ) = 6.283 meters, which equals exactly with twelve royal cubits (6.2832 m /
12 = 0.5236 m = 1 cubit). This means that there is a fixed mathematical connection
between modern meter and ancient Egyptian cubit through the geometry of a circle
divided by twelve.

In 1982 a German archeologist Rainer Stadelmann found broken pieces of a very old
pyramidion from Dahshur near the 4th true pyramid (also known as Red pyramid of
Snefru). In a book called: Egypt: The World of the Pharaohs there is a picture of this
pyramidion with a caption:

"The pyramidion from the Red Pyramid of Snefru
North Dahshur; Fourth Dynasty, ca. 2605 BC; limestone; H. 100cm W. 157cm.

The capstone of the pyramid was found broken into pieces in the rubble by the cast side and reassembled. It is the only surviving pyramidion from a pyramid tomb of the Old Kingdom, and may have been covered with sheet metal."

Notice the height and the width of the pyramidion: "H. 100cm W. 157cm".

The height of the found pyramidion was exactly one meter and the perimeter (1.57 m x 4 = 6.283 meters) exactly 12 cubits long. This pyramidion had the same relationship between height and width than the Great Pyramid of Giza.

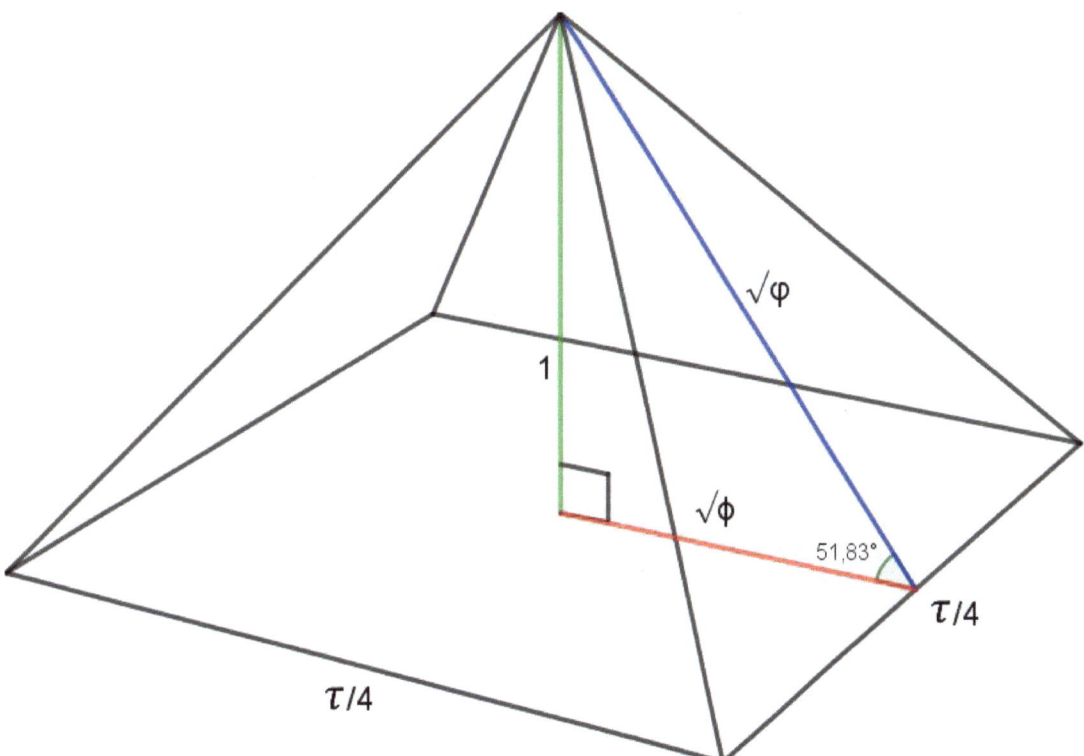

The dimension of the Dahshur's pyramidion in meters. Height: 1 meter (1.91 cubits). Side length: 1.57 meters x 4 sides = 6.28 meters (3 cubits x 4 sides = 12 cubits). These dimensions correspond the geometry of the 1st true pyramid (The Great Pyramid of Giza). The ratio between the overall length of the square base (6.283 meters) and height of the pyramidion (1 m) corresponds the ratio of 2π or τ. At the same time the structure represents the square roots of the golden ratios √ϕ (0.786) and √φ (1.272) as shown in the picture above. The geometry and the dimensions of this pyramidion holds a key for four different mathematically interesting concepts: the geometry of a circle (divided by twelve), the golden ratio, the length of a meter and the length of a cubit - all fitted into the same geometry.

It has been known at least for centuries that the dimensions of the Great Pyramid (the relationship between the circumference of its square base and its height) represents very accurately the geometry of a circle. If the height of the pyramid is one (representing the radius), then the square base of the pyramid corresponds the circumference of a circle $2\pi = 6.283$. Still, hardly anyone could have imagined that one day one would find some 5,000 year old scale model of the Great Pyramid with a height of exactly 1 meter and with a circumference of the base exactly 12 cubits long – as if it was built in our time using the knowledge of our metric system and its connection to ancient cubit through the geometry of a circle. The shape of this pyramidion is a perfect representation of four mathematically very interesting concepts: the geometry of a circle divided by twelve, the golden ratio, the length of a meter and the length of a cubit – all included into one and the same geometry.

The length of one meter was originally determined by the circumference of the globe. This definition was made in France at the turn of the 18th and 19th century amidst the French Revolution. One meter was originally defined to be one ten millionth of the distance between the North Pole and the Equator through Paris (10,000,000 meters x 10^{-7} = 1 meter). The distance covers one quarter of the Earth's circumference. Therefore, four quarters – full circle – equals 40,000,000 meters, which is the circumference of the Earth.

However, the idea of establishing a system of measurement based on the dimensions of the globe did not initially come from France but was much earlier origin. According to very old texts, the ancient Egyptian unit of measurement (royal cubit), by which all the true pyramids of Egypt were built, was originally derived from the dimensions of the Earth. That is why many widely respected scholars throughout the history of science, Isaac Newton among them, used considerable amount of time and resources to determine the exact length of the ancient Egyptian cubit. It was said that great knowledge was encrypted into this measure and into the structures built using this measure.

Ground Plan of Giza

As one is viewing the three Giza pyramids from above with the Google Earth Map Tool, one may feel the urge to draw them inside a rectangle with a ruler tool. This would not be possible if the pyramids were not aligned precisely according to the four cardinal points of compass. For example, the four sides of the 1st true pyramid are oriented towards the north, south, east and west with an accuracy of up to about 99.95 %. Smooth sides and nearly perfect 90-degree angles create a readymade basis for drawing the ground plan visible.

When examining the side lengths and the diagonal of the Ground Plan of Giza in cubits, a clear mathematical pattern emerges. The width, the length and the diagonal can be expressed respectively in a form of a square roots of 2, 3 and 5 multiplied by a thousand. Measurement results match mathematical values with up to about 99.9 % accuracy.

The Ground Plan of Giza:

East-west width: $\sqrt{2}$ x 1,000 = 1,414.2 cubits (740.5 meters).

North-south length: $\sqrt{3}$ x 1,000 = 1,732.1 cubits (906.9 meters).

Diagonal: $\sqrt{5}$ x 1,000 = 2,236.1 cubits (1,170.8 meters).

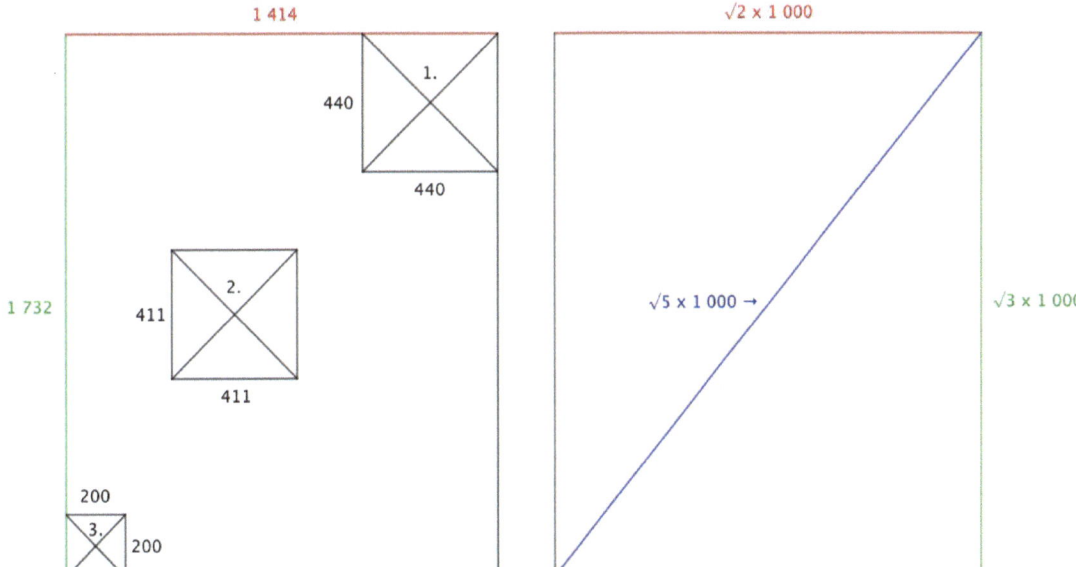

On the left, the Ground Plan of Giza, and its dimensions in cubits. On the right are the same numbers expressed mathematically in a form of square root and a multiplier.

The probability of constructing a pyramid ground plan with a side length of $\sqrt{2}$ x 1,000 cubits with an accuracy of 99,9% purely by chance, is totally possible. This can happen just by a coincidence, and there is nothing very special about it. But if also the another side length of the ground plan together with the diagonal of the same ground plan happens to represent this same mathematical phenomena ($\sqrt{3}$ x 1,000 and $\sqrt{5}$ x 1,000 cubits) with the same accuracy, suddenly the probability of chance drops drastically.

History, however, is very reluctant to correct itself on the basis of mathematical probabilities. Thus, if we want to use mathematics to prove the inconsistency of the prevailing historical truth, then the evidence must be exceptionally strong. For this purpose, we must travel from Giza some 20 kilometers southeast to a place called Dahshur, where we can find two more true pyramids. We go there to find out whether this mathematical phenomenon found in Giza is purely coincidental or whether it was done intentionally. For if it was intentional, then this same phenomenon would most likely be found also from the Ground Plan of Dahshur. Otherwise, the side lengths of the Ground Plan of Dahshur would be just some random numbers without any indication of a mathematical purpose.

Ground Plan of Dahshur

Two lesser-known true pyramids are located in Dahshur, about twenty kilometers southeast from the Giza pyramids. Both of the Dahshur pyramids are of equal height: about 200 cubits or 105 meters tall. They are built more than two kilometers apart from each other in the middle of a desert with no apparent reason or purpose.

The appearance of the northern of these two pyramids (4th pyramid) closely resembles the Giza pyramids, even though its slope is less steep. Instead, the appearance of the 5th pyramid is quite different from any other true pyramid. Its geometry is twofold: the bottom part of the pyramid is much steeper than the top part. The bending point is located at approximately 90 cubits (47 meters) high from the ground. Because of its shape, the 5th pyramid is also known as the Bent Pyramid.

Just like the pyramids of Giza, both Dahshur pyramids are also aligned with great precision along with the four cardinal points of compass. When surveying the Ground Plan of Dahshur, its dimensions proves to be very accurately 1,000 cubits (523.6 meters) wide and 4,270.57 cubits (2,236 meters) long.

The Ground Plan of Dahshur:
East-west width: $\sqrt{1}$ x 1,000 = 1,000 cubits (523.6 meters).
North-south length: $\sqrt{5}$ x 1,000 = 2,236 meters (4,270.57 cubits).

The width of the Ground Plan of Dahshur is an even number in cubits, which is a clear sign of intentionality. As we compare this length to the side lengths of the Giza Ground Plan, we realize how nicely it fits to the bigger picture. From Giza Ground Plan we have already found three significant mathematical figures: $\sqrt{2}$, $\sqrt{3}$ and $\sqrt{5}$ multiplied by thousand. Now we found yet another number – number 1 multiplied by thousand. Because the number 1 can also be written in a form of: $\sqrt{1}$, the pattern is clear: there always seems to be a square root of a whole number with a multiplier of one thousand.

The north-south length of the ground plan is very precisely 2,236 meters, which in turn corresponds to $\sqrt{5}$ in meters: $\sqrt{5}$ x 1,000 = 2,236 meters = 4,270.57 cubits. The

15

expression: √5 x 1,000 = 2,236 is already familiar from Giza, where it acts as a diagonal of the Giza Ground Plan. However, the diagonal of the Ground Plan of Giza is √5 x 1,000 cubits, but here we have it in meters. Could the use of meters be intentional? Well, this is not the first time we encounter this phenomenon. It reminds us of the capstone found by Rainer Stadelmann, which also worked in meters and in cubits at the same time. But of course, we need yet more evidence to say, whether this was done intentionally.

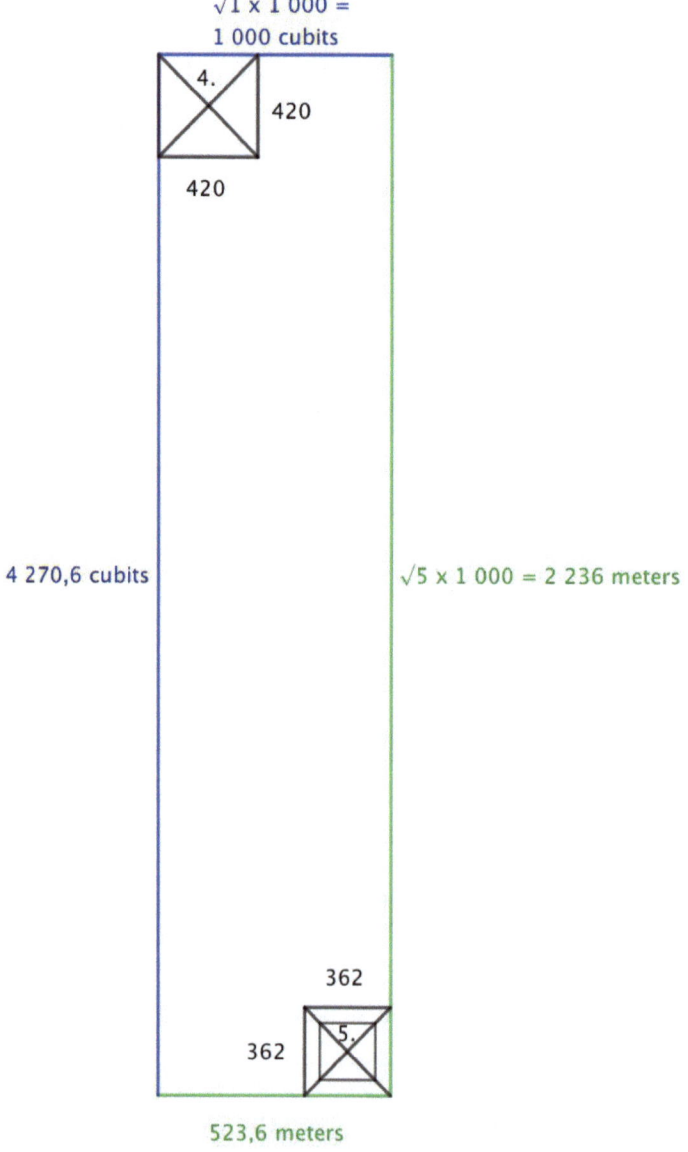

The Ground Plan of Dahshur (pyramids 4 and 5). The length of the ground plan: √5 x 1,000 = 2,236 meters. The width of the ground plan: √1 x 1,000 = 1,000 cubits. The same mathematical pattern emerges in both Giza and Dahshur Ground Plans: a square root of a whole number with a multiplier of 1,000.

The Great Ground Plan

So far, we have drawn and measured the ground plans of both, the Giza and the Dahshur pyramid areas, and in both cases our observations have supported the view that the architecture of these ground plans is based on carefully considered design. By studying these two ground plans, we can create a hypothesis from which we can try to predict the design of the third ground plan, the Great Ground Plan, which covers all five true pyramids.

If the placement of each five true pyramids on a map really follows some greater mathematical plan, then this should also be seen from the Great Ground Plan. However, this time the area is considerably larger than before (some 10 times larger), so presumably the multiplier is also correspondingly bigger.

Based on our prior knowledge from the Giza and Dahshur's ground plans, we can expect the Great Ground Plan to exhibit at least some of the following features:

1. We expect to find side lengths that consist of square root of whole numbers with a multiplier of 1,000 or 10,000. For example: ($\sqrt{5}$ x 1,000 or $\sqrt{5}$ x 10,000).

2. We expect to find usage of meters and cubits simultaneously (like in the case of Ground Plan of Dahshur or in the case of pyramidion found from Dahshur).

3. We expect the results to show with very high accuracy. In practice, this means an accuracy of about 99.9 %.

Once the conditions are set, we begin to draw the Great Ground Plan visible according to the outer borders of the Giza and Dahshur Ground Plans.

The east-west length of the Great Ground Plan fits perfectly with our expectations. The length is 8,000 meters (15,278.8 cubits) long, with an accuracy of 99.98 %. 8,000 meters is a round number that can be expressed in a form of $\sqrt{64}$ x 1,000 meters.

However, when determining the north-south length of the Great Ground Plan, we encounter a strange and unpredictable phenomenon. The ground plan is very precisely

40,000 cubits long, but only if we use the northeast corner of the 5th pyramid as the corner point instead of the default southeast corner. When we do this, the ground plan will be approximately 99.92 % accurate to 40,000 cubits (20,944 meters). The diagonal of the Great Ground Plan, on the other hand, becomes $\sqrt{5}$ x 10,000 = 22,360.68 meters long (with an accuracy of 99.97 %), but only if we are aiming to the northwest corner of the 5th true pyramid.

The phenomenon seems to be systematic: The southeast corner of the 5th pyramid defines the southern and eastern boundaries of the Ground Plan of Dahshur. The northeast corner of the 5th pyramid defines the southern and eastern borders of the Great Ground Plan. The northwest corner of the 5th pyramid defines the diagonal of the Great Ground Plan. The architect has made the 5th pyramid, the so-called Bent Pyramid, kind of a cornerstone for both of these ground plans, with each corner having its own specific measuring purposes. Later in this study, we will take a closer look at the geometry of the 5th pyramid itself.

To sum up the results:
- The east-west width of the Great Ground Plan is 8,000 meters. This is an even number that can be expressed in a form of $\sqrt{64}$ x 1,000 meters with an accuracy of 99.98 %.
- The north-south length of the Great Ground Plan is 40,000 cubits, that can be expressed in a form of $\sqrt{16}$ x 10,000 cubits with an accuracy of 99.92 %.
- The diagonal of the Great Ground Plan is $\sqrt{5}$ x 10,000 meters long with an accuracy of 99.97 %.
- The 5th pyramid acts as a cornerstone for all these results.

The survey exceeds all expectations but does so in an unpredictable way. Suddenly all the attention is drawn to the 5th pyramid. The Bent Pyramid rises to a special position in defining the dimensions of the ground plans. Despite the long distances, the measurement results are extremely accurate. When measuring the 40,000 cubits or 20,944 meters long north-south border of the Great Ground Plan, the error is merely some 16 meters (99.92 % accuracy). On average, however, the measurement results are even more accurate. For example, when measuring the diagonal of the Great

Ground Plan, the accuracy is up to 99.97 %. This means an error of only about 6 meters for the entire 22,360 meters long diagonal. Given the enormous proportions of the true pyramids and the vast distances between the points to be measured, there is virtually no error at all.

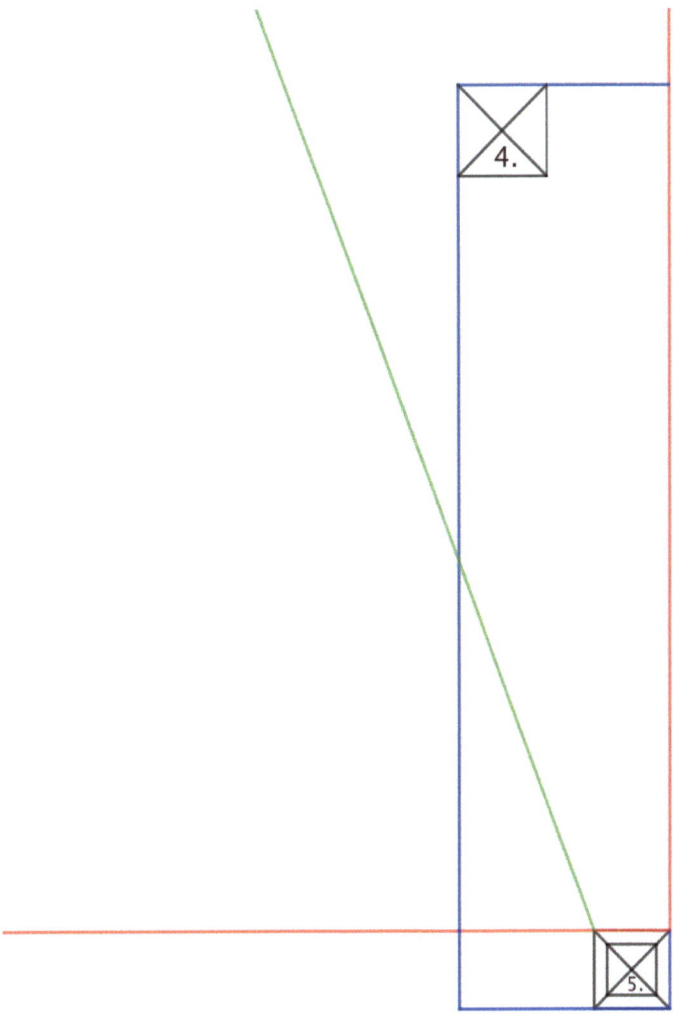

Southeast corner of the Great Ground Plan and the Ground Plan of Dahshur seen from above. The northeast, southeast and northwest corners of the 5th pyramid each have their own measuring purposes. Drawn in red the southeast corner of the Great Ground Plan, defined by the northeast corner of the 5th pyramid as shown. Drawn in green the diagonal of the Great Ground Plan, defined by the northwest corner of the 5th pyramid. Drawn in blue the Ground Plan of Dahshur, defined by the southeast corner of the 5th pyramid.

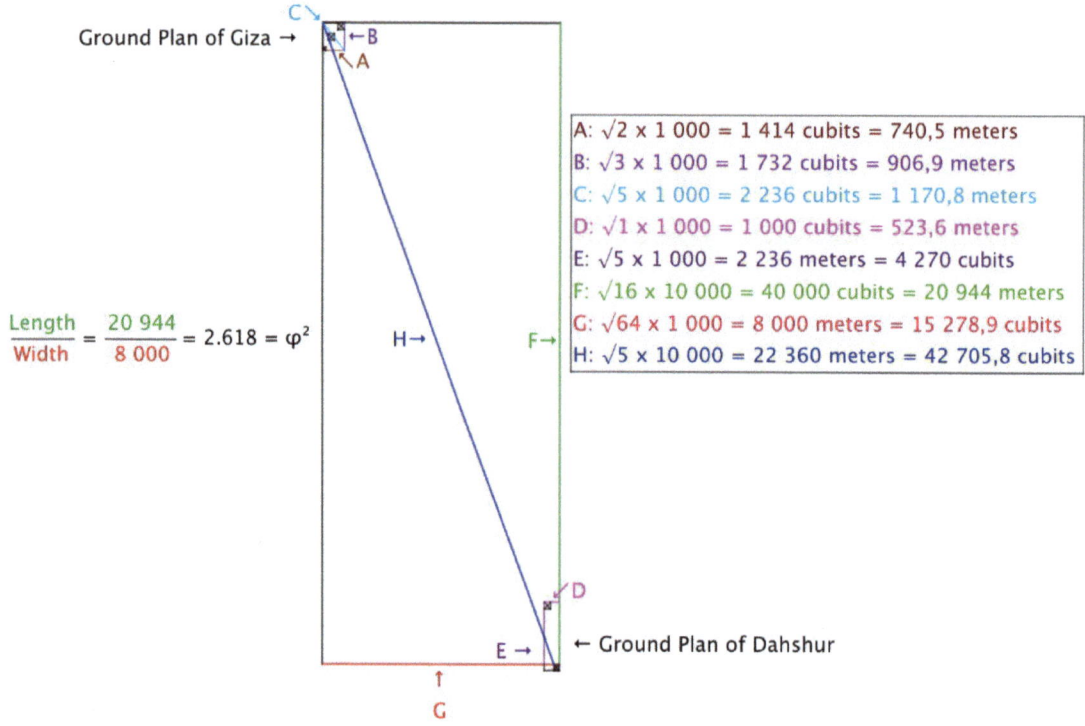

Ground Plan of Giza →

A: √2 x 1 000 = 1 414 cubits = 740,5 meters
B: √3 x 1 000 = 1 732 cubits = 906,9 meters
C: √5 x 1 000 = 2 236 cubits = 1 170,8 meters
D: √1 x 1 000 = 1 000 cubits = 523,6 meters
E: √5 x 1 000 = 2 236 meters = 4 270 cubits
F: √16 x 10 000 = 40 000 cubits = 20 944 meters
G: √64 x 1 000 = 8 000 meters = 15 278,9 cubits
H: √5 x 10 000 = 22 360 meters = 42 705,8 cubits

$$\frac{Length}{Width} = \frac{20\ 944}{8\ 000} = 2.618 = \varphi^2$$

← Ground Plan of Dahshur

The Great Ground Plan (including the Ground Plan of Giza and the Ground Plan of Dahshur) with its main dimensions depicted in the same drawing. All of the 8 side lengths represent the same mathematical pattern. There is a whole number squared and then there is a multiplier of – either one thousand or ten thousand. This pattern works either in meters or in cubits. A total of 8 side lengths were found following the given formula. Five of them are designed primarily in cubits (A, B, C, D and F) and three of them in meters (E, G and H). In addition, the ratio between the length and the width of the Great Ground Plan forms a ratio of φ² or $\frac{5}{12}\tau \approx 2.618$, creating a link between the golden ratio and the ratio of pi which both are represented in the geometry of the Dahshur pyramidion and 1ˢᵗ true pyramid.

The ratio between the length and the width of the Great Ground Plan gives an approximation of the golden ratio known from the geometry of a circle:

20,944 meters / 8,000 meters = 2.618 $\approx \varphi^2$

Dividing the circle of 360 degrees with the ratio of φ², gives the so-called golden angle of 137.508°. If one is interested in seeing, how the ratio of φ² manifests in the divine design of nature, I recommend making a Google search for videos called: Nature by Numbers and Infinite Patterns by Cristóbal Vila.

20

Ground plan	Line	Square roots	Cubits	Meters
Giza	A	√2 x 1000	1 414,21	740,48
	B	√3 x 1000	1 732,05	906,90
	C	√5 x 1000	2 236,07	1 170,80
Dahshur	D	√1 x 1000	1 000,00	523,60
	E	√5 x 1000	4 270,58	2 236,07
Great	F	√16 x 10 000	40 000,00	20 943,95
	G	√64 x 1 000	15 278,87	8 000,00
	H	√5 x 10 000	42 705,75	22 360,68

Summary of the measurement results. A total of 8 side lengths were found following the given formula. Five of them are designed primarily in cubits (A, B, C, D and F) and three of them in meters (E, G and H). Cubits are written in blue and meters are written in green.

For anyone with prior knowledge of the architecture of the Great Pyramid, the use of square roots in ground plan architecture may not be such a big surprise. For example, it has long been known that the spatial design of the so-called King's Chamber of the Great Pyramid is designed to be best expressed in terms of square roots in cubits. But it may come as a surprise to many that the same design can also be expressed in meters using the ratio of φ^2 or $\frac{5}{12}\tau \approx 2.618$, as can be seen from the following picture taken from my previous study. This ratio of 2.618 is so often found all over the design of true pyramids that it is only appropriate to find it also from the ratio between the height and the width of the Great Ground Plan.

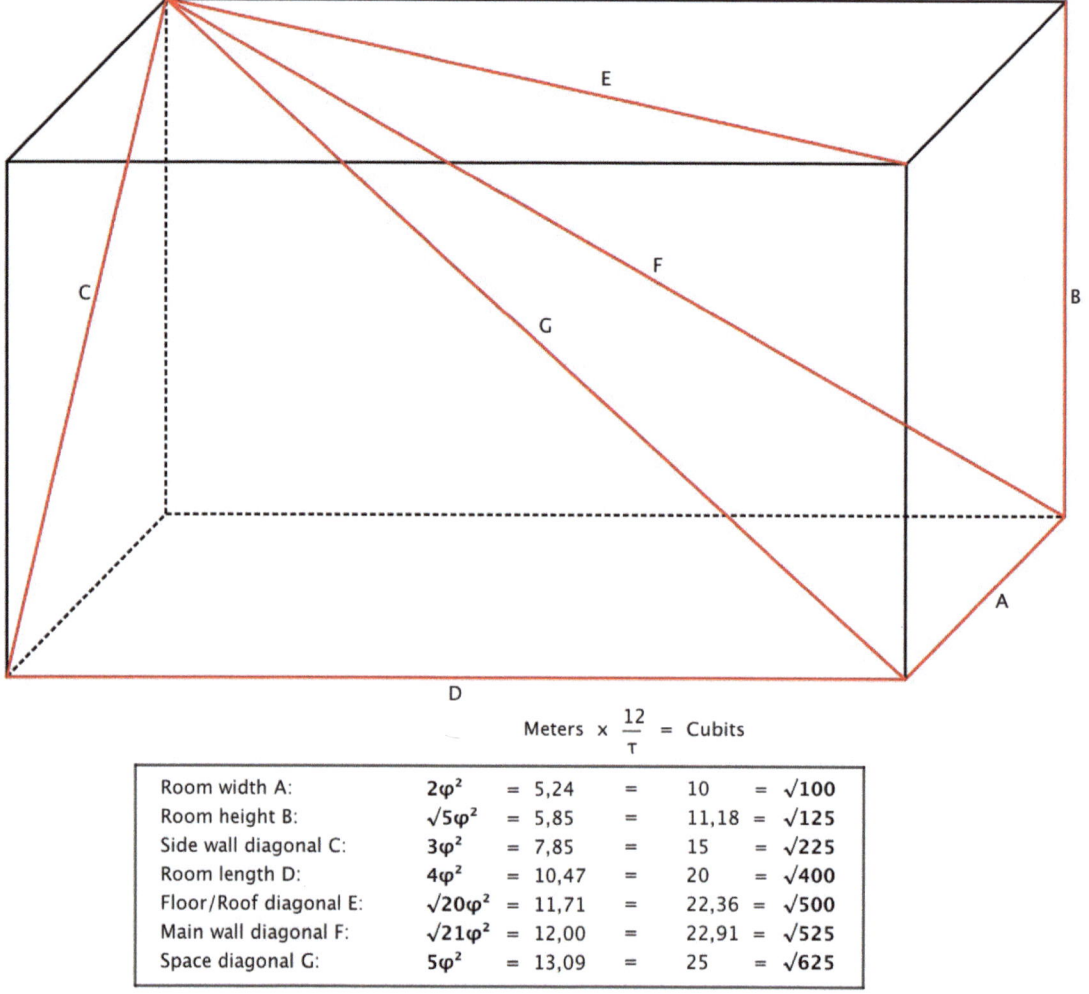

Meters	x $\frac{12}{\tau}$	= Cubits		
Room width A:	$2\varphi^2$ = 5,24	=	10	= $\sqrt{100}$
Room height B:	$\sqrt{5}\varphi^2$ = 5,85	=	11,18	= $\sqrt{125}$
Side wall diagonal C:	$3\varphi^2$ = 7,85	=	15	= $\sqrt{225}$
Room length D:	$4\varphi^2$ = 10,47	=	20	= $\sqrt{400}$
Floor/Roof diagonal E:	$\sqrt{20}\varphi^2$ = 11,71	=	22,36	= $\sqrt{500}$
Main wall diagonal F:	$\sqrt{21}\varphi^2$ = 12,00	=	22,91	= $\sqrt{525}$
Space diagonal G:	$5\varphi^2$ = 13,09	=	25	= $\sqrt{625}$

The picture shows all main dimensions that can be found inside the King's Chamber of the Great Pyramid. The table below the picture shows the length of each line both in meters and in cubits. The cubits are best expressed as the square roots of a whole number. The meters, in turn, are best expressed through the ratio of φ^2 or $\frac{5}{12}\tau \approx 2.618$.

It is precisely the ratio of 2.618 that links the golden ratio, the cubit, the meter and the geometry of a circle divided by twelve together:

5 cubits = φ^2 or $\frac{5}{12}\tau$ meters.

In this study I prefer using φ^2 instead of $\frac{5}{12}\tau$ just because φ^2 is easier and simpler to write. However, φ^2 and $\frac{5}{12}\tau$ are interchangeable, so one can use either one.

22

Key Coordinates

A total of 12 different coordinates are required to define the whole Great Ground Plan and its 8 mathematically significant side lengths or diagonals.

<u>Corners of the Giza Ground Plan:</u>

North-east corner of the Giza Ground Plan: 29.980181°, 31.135375°

South-east corner of the Giza Ground Plan: 29.972003°, 31.135375°

South-west corner of the Giza Ground Plan: 29.972003°, 31.127704°

North-west corner of the Giza Ground Plan: 29.980181°, 31.127704°

<u>Corners of the Dahshur Ground Plan:</u>

North-east corner of the Dahshur Ground Plan: 29.809540°, 31.210427°

South-east corner of the Dahshur Ground Plan: 29.789369°, 31.210427°

South-west corner of the Dahshur Ground Plan: 29.789369°, 31.205011°

North-west corner of the Dahshur Ground Plan: 29.809540°, 31.205011°

<u>Corners of the Great Ground Plan:</u>

North-east corner of the Great Ground Plan: 29.980155°, 31.210601°

South-east corner of the Great Ground Plan: 29.791078°, 31.210427°

South-west corner of the Great Ground Plan: 29.791059°, 31.127702°

North-west corner of the Great Ground Plan: 29.980181°, 31.127704°

<u>Corners of the 5th true pyramid:</u>

North-east corner of the 5th pyramid: 29.791078°, 31.210427°

South-east corner of the 5th pyramid: 29.789369°, 31.210427°

South-west corner of the 5th pyramid: 29.789369°, 31.208466°

North-west corner of the 5th pyramid: 29.791078°, 31.208466°

Geometry of the 5th True Pyramid

The geometry of the 5th true pyramid is an interesting exception compared to all other true pyramids in Egypt. Instead of uniformly tapered profile towards the top of a square-based pyramid, this 200-cubit high pyramid giant is steeper at the bottom than at the top. The bending point is located at an altitude of about 90 cubits (47 meters).

According to the prevailing theory, the 5th pyramid was originally supposed to rise at the slope of its lower part all the way to the top, but due to the cracks observed in the structure, the architect decided to change the plans during the process and built the upper part of the pyramid more gentle. Because of this, the Bent Pyramid has been regarded as a failed pyramid. It was said, that it was abandoned by the builders as soon as it was completed, and that the builders built another pyramid (the 4th pyramid) to replace it.

However, mathematical analysis of the Bent Pyramid shows that the structure of the 5th pyramid is anything but failed. The Bent Pyramid has stood the test of time well. Its overall structure is still largely intact, and it still has large part of its casing stones in place – unlike almost all the other true pyramids. While the pyramids of Giza have attracted all the attention of the researchers and tourists throughout the millennia, in the meantime the pyramids of Dahshur have been allowed to stand in much greater peace and serenity.

The first thing that catches the eye of a mathematical observer is the 5th pyramid's bending. With prior knowledge from the ground plans the breakthrough comes quite quickly. If the study of the ground plans has taught us anything, it has taught us to look for the square roots. The geometry of the Bent Pyramid follows very beautifully the square roots of 1, 2, 3 and 4. This becomes evident as we take a closer look at the corners of the 5th true pyramid.

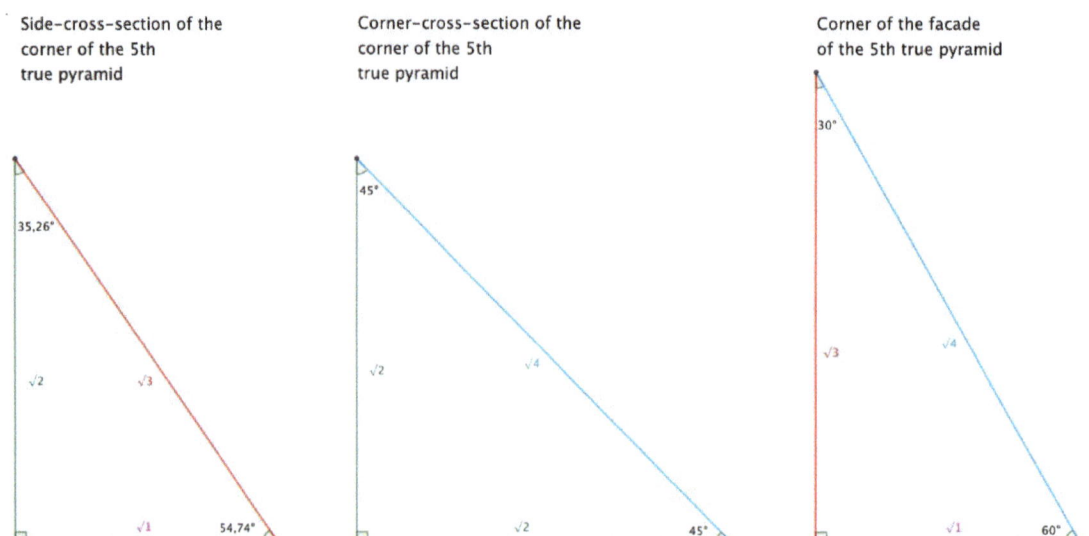

Side-cross-section of the corner of the 5th true pyramid

Corner-cross-section of the corner of the 5th true pyramid

Corner of the facade of the 5th true pyramid

The corners of the 5ᵗʰ pyramid are built by using side lengths of: √1, √2, √3, √4. Also, four precisely determined angles can be found: 30°, 45°, 60°, 90°. All of this demonstrates intentionality, exceptional architectural skill and mathematical design.

All side lengths of the 5ᵗʰ pyramid can be expressed in square roots, as can be seen from the picture on the next page. They can be expressed both in cubits and in meters by applying the following rule of calculation:

The rule of calculation for the 5ᵗʰ true pyramid:

For meters: 1/3 x sqrt () x 100
For cubits: 2/π x sqrt () x 100,

where "sqrt ()" means square root. Inside the parentheses comes the number from which the square root is taken. All the needed square roots can be found from the figure below. With this knowledge we can calculate all side lengths of the 5ᵗʰ true pyramid both in meters and in cubits.

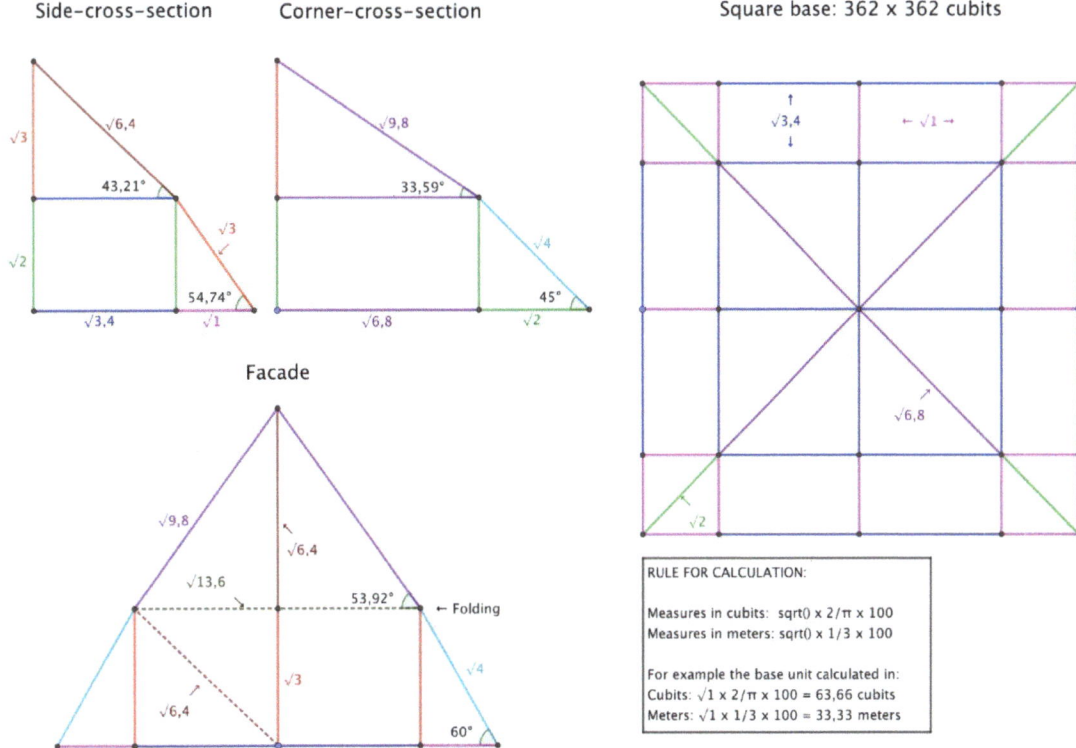

Side-cross-section Corner-cross-section Square base: 362 x 362 cubits

Facade

RULE FOR CALCULATION:

Measures in cubits: sqrt() x 2/π x 100
Measures in meters: sqrt() x 1/3 x 100

For example the base unit calculated in:
Cubits: √1 x 2/π x 100 = 63,66 cubits
Meters: √1 x 1/3 x 100 = 33,33 meters

The figure shows the cross-sections, the façade and the square base of the 5ᵗʰ true pyramid. All the dimensions can be expressed in square roots. The length of the unit side (1) is 63.66 cubits, or 33.33 meters. The table attached shows the rule of calculation for calculating the side lengths of the Bent Pyramid in both meters and in cubits.

The four most important side lengths calculated in meters and in cubits:

In meters:

$\sqrt{1}$ x 1/3 x 100 = 33.33 meters
$\sqrt{2}$ x 1/3 x 100 = 47.14 meters
$\sqrt{3}$ x 1/3 x 100 = 57.74 meters
$\sqrt{4}$ x 1/3 x 100 = 66.67 meters

In cubits:

$\sqrt{1}$ x 2/π x 100 = 63.66 cubits
$\sqrt{2}$ x 2/π x 100 = 90.03 cubits
$\sqrt{3}$ x 2/π x 100 = 110.27 cubits
$\sqrt{4}$ x 2/π x 100 = 127.32 cubits

27

When calculating meters, we are using the ratio of 1/3 = 0.3333… and when calculating cubits, we are using the ratio of 2/π = 0.6366... When dividing these ratios with each other, we determine the relationship between meter and cubit:

1 cubit equals $\frac{1/3}{2/\pi}$ = 0.5236 meters and 1 meter equals $\frac{2/\pi}{1/3}$ = 1.9099 cubits.

From all of these lengths, the most interesting is undoubtedly the unit side length (1): 63.66 cubits, or 33.33 meters, which can be derived directly from the 1/12th of the Earth's circumference, as demonstrated in the picture below.

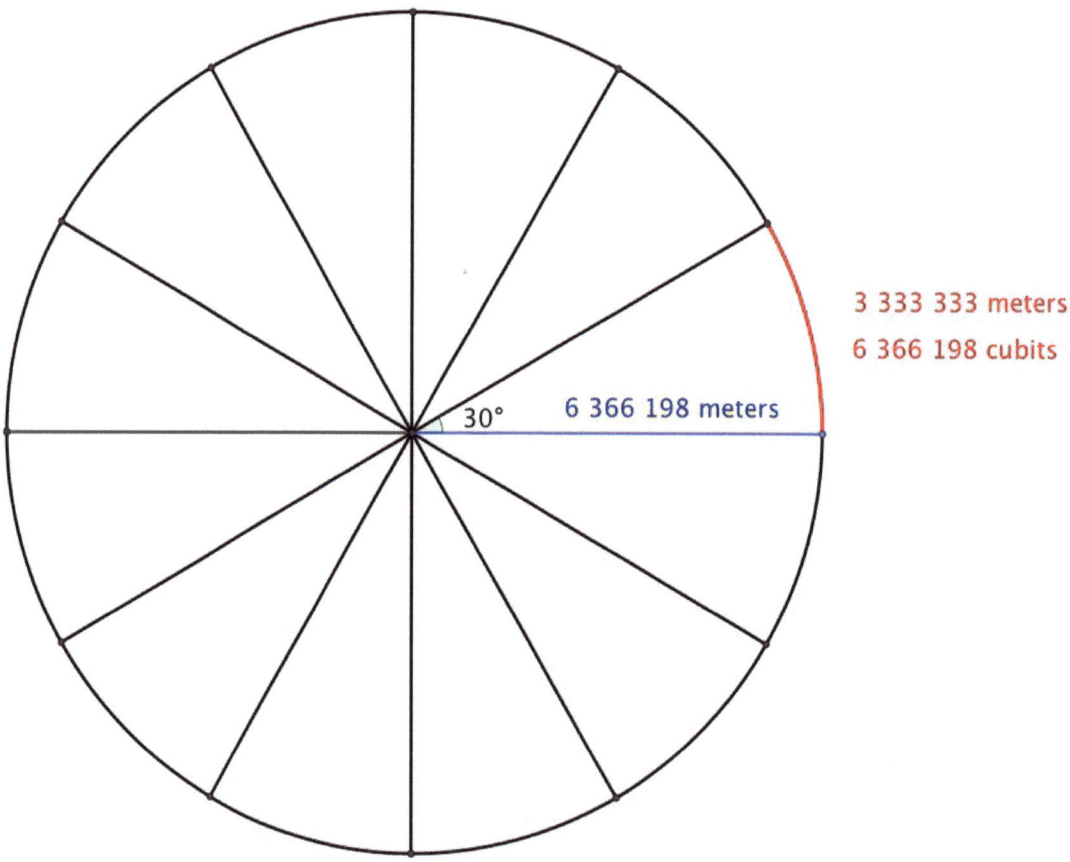

Radius of the Earth = 6 366 198 m
Circumference of the Earth = 6 366 198 m x τ = 40 000 000 m
1/12th of the circumference of the Earth:
40 000 000 / 12 = 3 333 333 meters
40 000 000 / 12 / (τ/12) = 6 366 198 cubits

3 333 333 meters
6 366 198 cubits

6 366 198 meters

30°

The coefficients used in the rule of calculation of the 5th true pyramid can be derived directly from the 1/12th of the Earth's circumference by multiplying results by 10⁻⁷.

The radius of the Earth is about 6,366,198 meters (12,158,542 cubits) and the circumference about 40,000,000 meters (76,394,373 cubits). Hence, the $1/12^{th}$ of the circumference of the Earth is:

40,000,000 meters / 12 = 3,333,333 meters

76,394,373 cubits / 12 = 6,366,198 cubits.

As mentioned earlier, the length of the base unit for length, the meter, was originally derived from the quarter of the Earth's perimeter multiplied by 10^{-7}. In this case, however, the base unit for length is not one-fourth of the Earth's perimeter, but one-twelfth of the Earth's perimeter. As we divide the result by 10 million (or multiply it by 10^{-7}), we get the coefficients for the rule of calculation.

Coefficient for meters: 40,000,000 / 12 x 10^{-7} = 0.3333... = 1/3
Coefficient for cubits: 76,394,372.68 / 12 x 10^{-7} = 0.6366... = 2/π

The proportions of the Earth are hidden in the Geometry of the 5th pyramid in the most elegant way imaginable: through the Earth's circumference divided by twelve.

After all, it seems that it was not the Great Pyramid into which the architect hid the direct information about the dimensions of the Earth. Instead, it was the fifth pyramid, which had been forgotten and overlooked by the scholars for millennia. But in this study the 5th pyramid stands out in the way I think it was designed to do – as the cornerstone of the Great Ground Plan.

Summary and Conclusions

Meter, Cubit and Circle Divided by Twelve:

Circle divided by twelve is a very old symbol of divine perfection and it bears a very special meaning in our culture, for example through zodiac, clock face, musical scale, calendar year, and so on.

Contrary to all expectations, the modern meter and the ancient Egyptian unit of measurement, the royal cubit, together reflects this same sacred division. For if we draw a circle with a radius of one meter, and we divide its circumference by twelve, we get exactly 12 cubits. In other words, the meter and the cubit are connected to each other through the geometry of a circle divided by twelve.

In 1982 a German archeologist Rainer Stadelmann found broken pieces of some 5,000-year-old pyramidion from Dahshur near the 4th true pyramid. This pyramidion had the same relationship between the height and width than the Great Pyramid of Giza, except that the height was exactly 1 meter and the total length of the perimeter was 12 cubits long. It seemed that the ancient architect had chosen these measures deliberately.

The shape and the dimensions of this pyramidion represents four very interesting mathematical ratios simultaneously: the geometry of a circle divided by twelve, the golden ratio, the meter, and the cubit. Whether all this was done intentionally or not, the shape of this pyramidion is a perfect representation of all these features.

Study of the Ground Plans

All true pyramids are aligned precisely according to the four cardinal points of compass. Smooth sides and nearly perfect 90-degree angles create a readymade basis for drawing the ground plans visible.

Ground Plan of Giza:

The width, the length, and the diagonal of the Ground Plan of Giza in cubits can be expressed as follows:

Width: $\sqrt{2}$ x 1,000 cubits.
Length: $\sqrt{3}$ x 1,000 cubits.
Diagonal: $\sqrt{5}$ x 1,000 cubits.

All these lengths seem to follow a certain mathematical pattern. If this pattern was made intentionally, it should also be found from the Ground Plan of Dahshur.

Ground Plan of Dahshur:

The same pattern can also be found in Dahshur, albeit with the exception that the north-south length of the Ground Plan of Dahshur follows the rule only in meters. Along with Stadelmann's pyramidion, this is the second time we find meters and cubits used together simultaneously.

Width: $\sqrt{1}$ x 1,000 cubits.
Length: $\sqrt{5}$ x 1,000 meters.

Now it seems confirmed that the side lengths of the ground plans follow a certain pattern: The square root of an integer multiplied by a thousand. This rule seems to apply both in meters and in cubits. But in order to be sure, we must draw yet one more ground plan to see if our hypothesis really works. For this purpose, we draw the Great Ground Plan encompassing all five true pyramids.

The Great Ground Plan:

Width: $\sqrt{64}$ x 1,000 meters = 8,000 meters.
Length: $\sqrt{16}$ x 10,000 cubits = 40,000 cubits.
Diagonal: $\sqrt{5}$ x 10,000 meters = 22,360.68 meters.

The length of the Great Ground plan is √16 x 10,000 cubits, the width √64 x 1,000 meters and the diagonal √5 x 10,000 meters long. The Great Ground Plan embodies beautiful mathematical design. The use of meters and cubits together proves to be intentional.

A special feature of the Great Ground Plan is the emphasis on the role of the 5th true pyramid (the so-called Bent Pyramid) as a cornerstone. All of its corners, except the southwest corner, has its own specific function in terms of measurements. The southeast corner of the 5th pyramid defines the southern and eastern boundaries of the Ground Plan of Dahshur. The northeast corner of the 5th pyramid defines the southern and eastern borders of the Great Ground Plan and the northwest corner of the 5th pyramid defines the diagonal of the Great Ground Plan.

The ratio between the length and the width of the Great Ground Plan is 20,943.6 m / 8,000 m = 2.618 = φ^2 = $\frac{5}{12}\tau$. This ratio can be expressed either through golden ratio (φ^2) or via value of pi: 5(π/6). In the geometry of a circle, the number 2.618 defines the golden angle: 360° / 2.618 = 137.5°. 2.618 meters is also equivalent to five cubits.

Geometry of the 5th True Pyramid

The side lengths of the corners of the 5th true pyramid are designed by using square roots of: √1, √2, √3, √4 and angles of 30°, 45°, 60°, 90°. All of this demonstrates highly advanced mathematical design, which is a clear sign of intentional planning.

The exact side-lengths of the 5th true pyramid can be calculated both in meters and in cubits by using the following rule of calculation. Sqrt() values can be found from the figure at the end of this book.

The rule of calculation:

For meters: 1/3 x sqrt () x 100
For cubits: 2/π x sqrt () x 100,

The coefficients (1/3 and 2/π) can be derived directly from the length of one-twelfth of the circumference of the Earth. Notice once again: the circle divided by twelve.

Coefficient for meters: $40,000,000 / 12 \times 10^{-7} = 0.3333\ldots = 1/3$

Coefficient for cubits: $76,394,372.68 / 12 \times 10^{-7} = 0.6366\ldots = 2/\pi$

Conclusions

Although it has long been known that the dimensions of the Ground Plan of Giza can be expressed in square roots of integers 2, 3, and 5, the intentionality of the phenomenon was never clarified. A comprehensive study on the subject was lacking.

Many factors, along with the enormous sizes of these structures, have hampered the study of the true pyramids of Egypt over the centuries and millennia. True pyramids have always located in quite hostile and dangerous areas, which have made them extremely difficult to reach. For thousands of years true pyramids were largely buried into sand, which made it impossible to measure their actual width and height, let alone their ground plans. The foundations of the pyramids of Giza, for example, were more or less covered with sand until the early 20th century.

For obvious reasons scholars have always been primarily interested in Giza pyramid area, which has made the Dahshur a secondary area of research. In the 20th century, the Dahshur pyramid area was inside a military zone for quite long time, which made the research of the Dahshur pyramids even more difficult. The survey of the ground plans, especially the Great Ground Plan, was not truly possible until the era of satellites. The study became possible only when free and highly advanced internet-based mapping tools became available to ordinary people just over a decade ago. All in all, the fact that it took almost 5,000 years to develop sufficiently accurate measuring devices only to measure and comprehend the accuracy of the whole pyramid construction, tells one something about the nature of these monuments.

True pyramids are the oldest, the largest, and yet mathematically and geometrically the most advanced structures ever built on Earth. They have stood the test of time throughout the whole written history of humankind remaining their original shape and thus conveying the timeless information of their advanced architecture over the millennia.

The study of the measures and the geometry of the 5th pyramid, as well as the use of meter and cubit, show us that the builder must have had very profound understanding of the dimensions of the Earth. The survey of the ground plans, on the other hand, affirms that the positioning of true pyramids follows extremely accurate and systematic mathematical plan. Therefore, we must conclude, that the true pyramids were not randomly placed. Instead their locations and architecture were carefully considered. These pyramids were not designed individually, at different times, or by different architects. Instead they form a single whole with a mathematical significance being a creation of one great architect.

True pyramids were never built as graves for pharaohs. Neither were they built for any other practical purposes. Rather they were built to represent a higher mathematical and geometrical knowledge, which was regarded as sacred, for it is the key for unlocking the holiest level of reality: the timeless and unchanging laws of nature.

In this chaotic world, where everything seems to be subject to change, the only truly stable level is hidden behind our senses. It can only be realized through human reason, described only through mathematics, and applied in practice only through geometry. This hidden level of reality is the basis of all our science and technology and thus all our well-being. It has always remained the same, and will always remain the same, forming the only true basis for a truly stable and prosperous society.

For thousands of years, humanity lacked this hidden and higher level of knowledge, exposing us to the forces of darkness and thus misery. But once the timeless level of reality was finally reached, just a few centuries ago, the whole new level of possibilities suddenly emerged. But this sacred level of reality is genuinely beneficial only when treated with the greatest respect, wisdom and care. Only then it will allow us to build a society upon truly solid basis and in harmony with nature. In the hands of fools, however, it will only reinforce the powers of chaos and destruction.

According to the ancient Egyptian mythology in the beginning, there was nothing but darkness and chaos, and out of these darkest waters the primordial hill arose, finally giving humanity a stable foundation for a new society. Who knows, perhaps myths like this were never meant to be mere myths, but rather symbolic descriptions of our ongoing journey through troubled times and prophecies for the time to come.

Epilogue

In summer 2016 Jacque Fresco, the founder of Venus project, received United Nation's award for his life's work. At the time of receiving the award, he was one hundred years old. Less than a year later he passed away.

His lifelong goal was to design nothing less, than a whole new foundation for human society based on perfect balance between humanity and nature through the use of modern science and technology.

I was deeply impressed by Jacque Fresco's thoughts and vision as I first got to know them more than a decade ago. His work served as a starting point for my own research. Now that my own research has finally been completed, I would like to draw attention back to the work of Jacque Fresco.

Jacque Fresco's approach was both practical and theoretical. On a practical level, he made blueprints and designed scale models of the future's prototype society down to the smallest detail. On a theoretical level, he lectured and wrote extensively on the problems of our current system, mainly concerning our current money-based planetary resource management system.

According to Jacque Fresco, the root cause of the overall imbalance of our modern society today, lies largely in our current global resource management system, which is based on our monetary system and market economy. The main ideology of market economy involves continuous economic growth and constantly increasing level of consumption, regardless of the burden inflicted on nature. In the long run this equation is practically impossible. At some point, we just need to start designing an entirely new resource management system, first for individual cities and later for the entire planet.

Current free market system is anything but smart resource management system for a finite planet. It is out of date and should be replaced by a more subtle, gentle and advanced system, based on scientific understanding of the workings of nature. According to Fresco, we should design a totally new global resource management system, that would be upgraded to the level of our contemporary scientific understanding of nature and wise management of Earth's resources. The model of society that Jacque Fresco spoke about for decades ago is, in modern terms, a perfect description of a circular economy.

With today's knowledge we could integrate human society into perfect balance with nature and build brand-new cities along these lines. Instead of money and politics, the decisions should be based on reason and science, to benefit all people.

With all the scientific knowledge and technological know-how we have gathered during the last few centuries, we could design genuinely fair and intelligent resource management system for our planet – a system that would be built upon the natural laws and natural order of things – instead of money, which is purely man made concept.

The idea itself is very interesting and inspiring, but all of this would require us to question much of our current culture and rethink many things inherited from our past in a whole new way. It would require detachment from contemporary culture and designing whole new way of life starting from scratch. Hence, there is a good reason to doubt whether such a society will ever really be possible, or whether it is once again another impossible utopia. It certainly would not suit for everyone, because the vast majority of people are so completely attached to this time and current culture, that they could not even consider the idea of living differently. But for a significant number of people it all would make sense. And therefore, I think the Jacque Fresco's ideas should be implemented in practice. In fact, I think it is our only chance.

The future of humanity looks rather bleak right now. It seems, that we have lost our ability to dream for the better future and by doing so, we are slowly but surely heading towards dystopia. For my part, if I had to make a choice between utopia and dystopia, I would definitely choose utopia, just because utopia includes hope. Hope, in turn, creates a fertile foundation for optimism and ingenuity. And when a large number of like-minded people come together and work towards a common goal, a positive chain reaction is most likely to happen, which ultimately makes utopia reality.

What we need now as a humanity is a genuine alternative for our current system. For one thing is certain: we cannot continue the way we are living right now for very much longer. We must change our ways, and the change must start right now.

A Few Pictures of the Book Enlarged:

Page 40: The Great Ground Plan

Page 41: The Corners of the 5th True Pyramid

Page 42: The Blueprint of the 5th True Pyramid and the Rule of Calculation

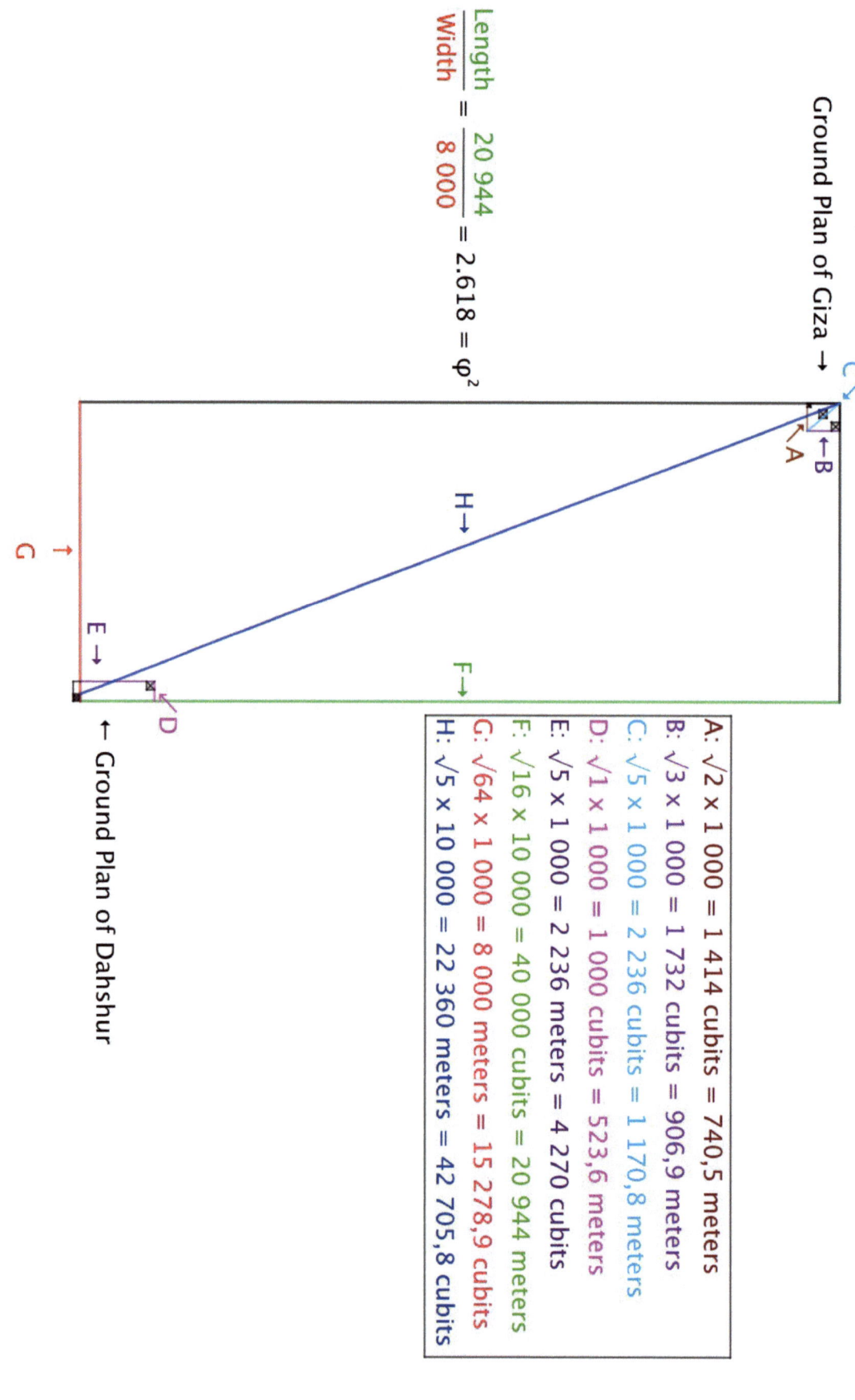

Ground Plan of Giza →

← Ground Plan of Dahshur

$$\frac{\text{Length}}{\text{Width}} = \frac{20\ 944}{8\ 000} = 2.618 = \varphi^2$$

A: √2 x 1 000 = 1 414 cubits = 740,5 meters
B: √3 x 1 000 = 1 732 cubits = 906,9 meters
C: √5 x 1 000 = 2 236 cubits = 1 170,8 meters
D: √1 x 1 000 = 1 000 cubits = 523,6 meters
E: √5 x 1 000 = 2 236 meters = 4 270 cubits
F: √16 x 10 000 = 40 000 cubits = 20 944 meters
G: √64 x 1 000 = 8 000 meters = 15 278,9 cubits
H: √5 x 10 000 = 22 360 meters = 42 705,8 cubits

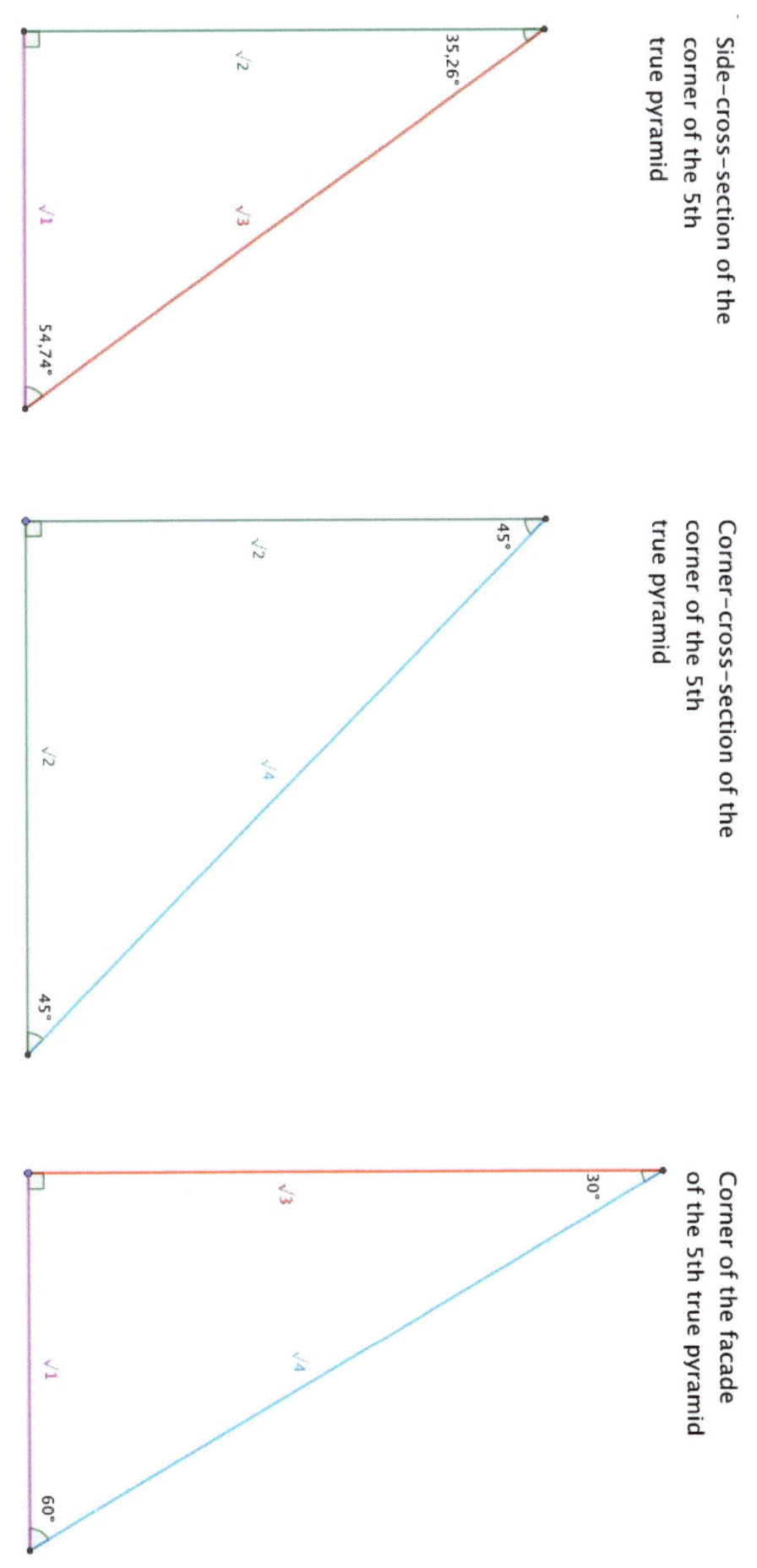

Side-cross-section of the corner of the 5th true pyramid

√2

√1

√3

35,26°

54,74°

Corner-cross-section of the corner of the 5th true pyramid

√2

√2

√4

45°

45°

Corner of the facade of the 5th true pyramid

√3

√1

√4

30°

60°

41

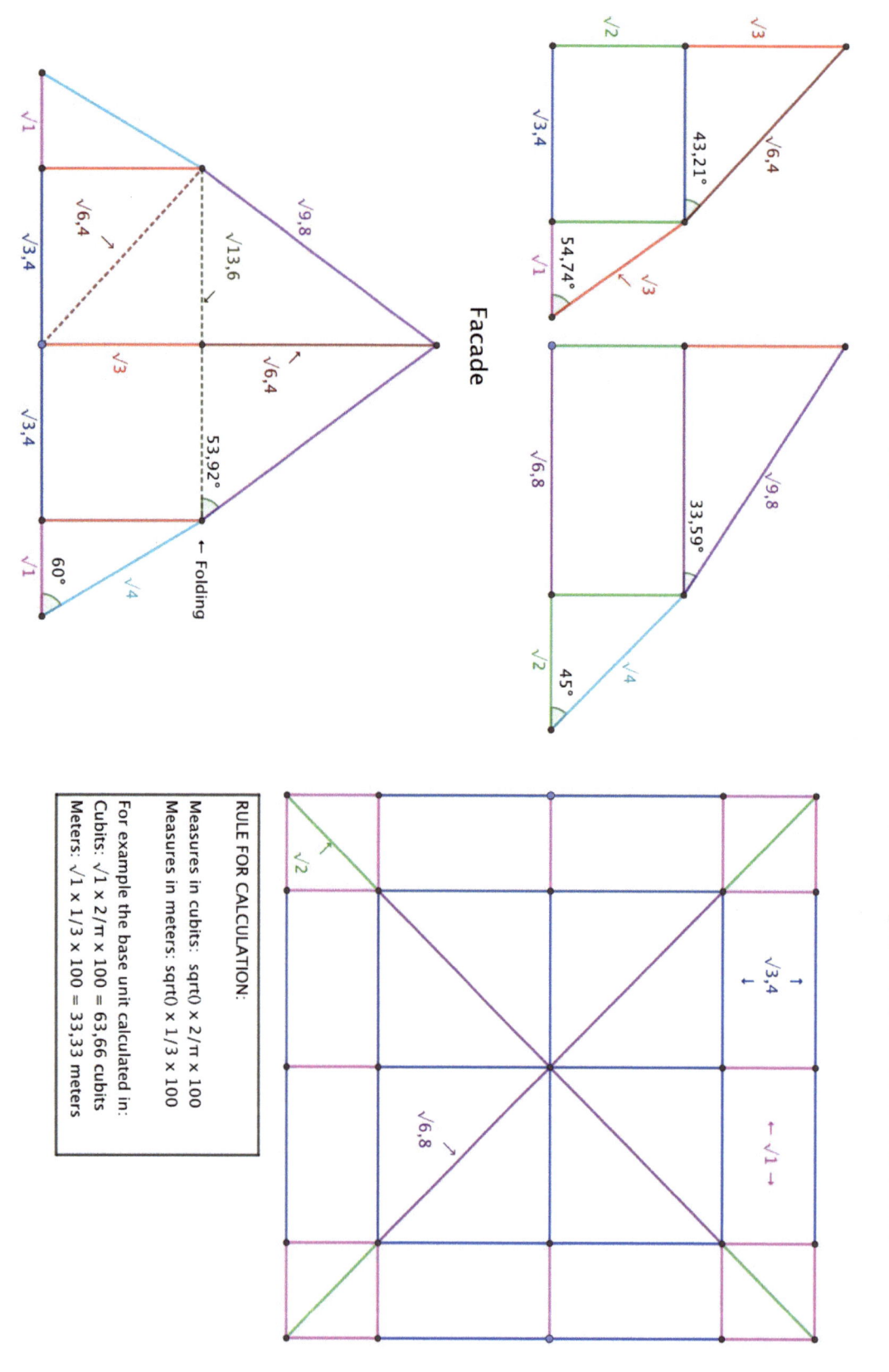

Side-cross-section

√3
√2
√3,4
43,21°
√6,4
54,74°
√3
√1

Corner-cross-section

√6,8
33,59°
√9,8
√2
√4
45°

Facade

√1
√6,4
√3,4
√3
√6,4
√13,6
√9,8
53,92°
← Folding
√3
√3,4
√1
60°
√4

Square base: 362 x 362 cubits

√2
√3,4
√1
√6,8

RULE FOR CALCULATION:

Measures in cubits: sqrt() x 2/π x 100
Measures in meters: sqrt() x 1/3 x 100

For example the base unit calculated in:
Cubits: √1 x 2/π x 100 = 63,66 cubits
Meters: √1 x 1/3 x 100 = 33,33 meters